b small publishing

MAD MACHINES
AND
DOTTY DEVICES

Susan Martineau

Illustrations by Martin Ursell

Published by b small publishing, Pinewood, 3a Coombe Ridings, Kingston upon Thames, Surrey KT2 7JT

© b small publishing, 2003

5 4 3 2

Colour reproduction: Vimnice International Ltd., Hong Kong.   Printed in Hong Kong by Wing King Tong

Editorial: Susan Martineau, Ronne Randall and Catherine Bruzzone *Design:* Louise Millar *Production:* Catherine Bruzzone and Madeleine Ehm

With thanks to Phil White, Head of Science, Grey Court School, Ham

ISBN 1 902915 91 7

British Library Cataloguing-in-Publication Data. A catalogue record for this book is available from the British Library.

Before You Begin

Most of the contraptions in this book are made with old stuff you will have around the house already. Don't forget to cover work surfaces with newspaper before you start, and clear up afterwards!

For the Whizzy Whirler on page 22 you will need to trace the template on to a piece of card. This is how to do it:

1 Trace the template shape using tracing paper, masking tape and a pencil.

2 Turn over the tracing paper and scribble over the lines with the pencil.

3 Turn the paper over again and tape it on to the card. Retrace over the lines.

boxes

plastic bottles

sticky tape

cardboard

polystyrene packing material

paper fasteners

paper-clips

straws

re-usable
sticky tack

drawing-pins

string and
thread

balloons

toilet roll tubes

electrical wire

glue

card

rubber bands

paper

old jam jars

marbles

clothes
pegs

scissors

mirrors

tracing paper

You will need a bit of grown-up help
in one or two places. These have been
marked with this special symbol.

3

Air Power

Blast Off!

This balloon rocket really whizzes along. You can use the same balloon again and again to show it off to your friends. You'll need a friend standing by to help set up the launch.

What you will need:
- 2 metres of string
- drinking straw
- chair
- balloon
- sticky tape
- clothes peg

1

Thread the straw on to the string. Tie one end to a door handle and the other to a chair.

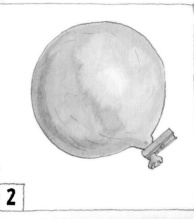

2

Place the chair so that the string is taut. Blow up the balloon and peg it closed.

3

Get a friend to help you tape the balloon on to the straw. Now unpeg the balloon and watch it go!

It's a Fact!

Isaac Newton's Third Law of Motion says that for every action there is an equal and opposite reaction. In this case, the air is pushed out of the back of the balloon and this 'action' makes the balloon move forwards, the 'opposite reaction'.

In a real rocket, fuel burns and makes hot gases which come rushing out of the back of the engine. This propels the rocket upwards.

You could tape a small box under the balloon for carrying 'cargo' – an empty matchbox is ideal.

Funky Fountains

Here are some fun fountains to make with your friends. Make a few and have a competition to see whose is best. You could add some food colouring to the water for extra fun. It's a good idea to do this outside!

What you will need:
- large, empty, plastic drinks bottle
- 2 bendy drinking straws
- plasticine or re-usable sticky tack

1

Remove any labels from the bottle. Half-fill the bottle with water.

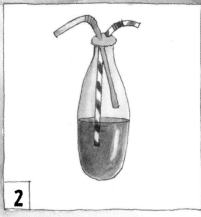

2

Put one straw into the water and position the other one so it is just above the water. Put some plasticine or sticky tack tightly round the mouth to make an airtight seal.

Blow!

3

Put the bottle into a sink or take it outside. Now blow into the straw which is not in the water.

See how powerful air can be by blowing through a straw at a paper boat!

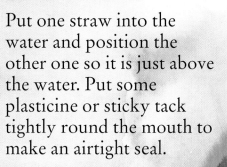

Rocket Man

Wernher von Braun (1912-1977) was a German inventor who longed to send a rocket to the moon. Unfortunately, during the Second World War (1939-1945) he was ordered to design rocket bombs instead. After the war he went to work in America and by the 1960s he was working at NASA (the US space programme). He led the team that launched the Saturn rockets which first took men to the moon.

It's a Fact!

When you blow air through a straw it squashes the air up – or compresses it. This makes the air more powerful. The air you blow into the bottle squashes up in the space above the water too and pushes the water up through the other straw.

5

Mighty Robot

Although this robot friend will not wash up for you or clean up your room he's fun to have around and will hold stuff for you. You can really go to town when adding buttons and features to your robot. These are just some ideas to get you started.

What you will need:
- 1 medium-sized box
- 1 small box
- kitchen foil
- sticky tape
- 6 toilet roll tubes
- scissors
- 3 glittery pipe cleaners
- sequins
- glue
- old pieces of polystyrene packing
- small bottle or carton lids
- old shiny sweet wrappers

1

Cover both the boxes with foil as if you were wrapping a present. Use sticky tape to secure the foil.

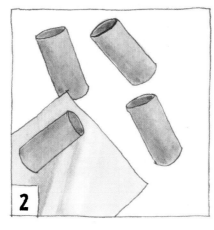

2

Cover 4 of the toilet roll tubes with foil and tuck the foil inside the ends.

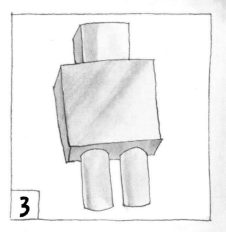

3

Tape the small box on top of the medium one. Then tape 2 of the covered tubes underneath for legs.

It's a Fact!

Robots are used in many industries on factory production lines. But they don't look at all like the artificial humans (androids) you see in films! They're really useful, though, and can do the jobs that humans would find very boring. In car manufacturing, robots weld together the steel panels to make the car body and then spray the body with several coats of paint.

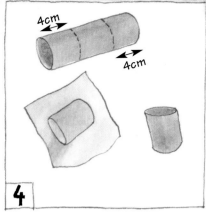

4 Cut 2 sections about 4 cm long from the ends of a remaining tube. Cover these with foil. Tuck in the ends.

5 Tape these on to the other 2 covered tubes to form 'hands'. Now tape these 'arms' on to the robot's body.

(!) **7** With adult help, use the scissors to pierce 3 holes in the top of the head.

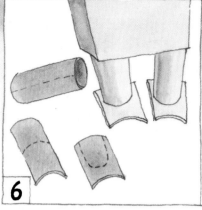

6 Cut the remaining tube in half lengthways. Cut 2 'feet' as shown. Cover these with foil. Tape on to the legs.

8 Curl the pipe cleaners around your finger and then push them through the holes.

9 Glue on sequins for eyes. Cover a piece of rectangular polystyrene with foil and stick on to make a mouth.

10 Cover lids with foil and sweet wrappers and stick on for buttons.

11 Use the arms and hands to keep pens, torches, hairbrushes or even your toothbrush tidy!

Androids in the Future?

Scientists are researching ways of making robots that can think for themselves and not have to be programmed before they perform certain tasks. Maybe one day you might have a robot around the house who will do the washing-up without having to be nagged!

Spyscope

Make a nifty periscope for peering over the fence at your neighbours! The sort of mirrors you need are small make-up ones which you can get from chemists' shops.

What you will need:
- 1 long, thin box about 24 cm long and 6 cm wide
- scissors and sticky tape
- 2 small rectangular mirrors about 6 cm x 8 cm

WARNING
Never point the Spyscope at the sun or you could damage your eyes.

1

Cut 2 slanting slits on one side of the box. Turn it over and cut 2 more. These should line up with the first slits.

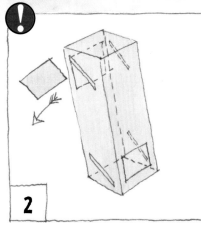

2

Cut 2 square windows in the box, as shown. They should line up with the slits.

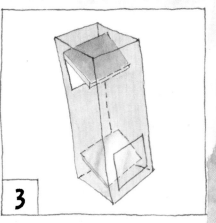

3

Slide the mirrors through the slits so that their reflective sides are facing each other. Use tape to fix them if necessary.

4

Hold one window to your face and look through. What can you see?

It's a Fact!

Light reflects, or bounces, from the top mirror to the bottom mirror. When you point the top mirror at something or someone, the light bouncing from it will then bounce down to the bottom mirror into your eyes and you will be able to see it!

Up Periscope!

Submarines use periscopes as their 'eyes'. Modern submarines have some really amazing periscopes with all kinds of special equipment. 'Attack' periscopes are really narrow at the top so that they cannot be seen by enemy radar. 'Search' periscopes are kitted out with cameras and night vision so that they can even be used when it's dark.

Anchors Aweigh!

Make yourself a speedy trimaran that will skim along in a breeze! You need to use the templates on the inside front cover. You could try making other boats too – maybe a catamaran with two hulls instead of three.

What you will need:

- 1 large polystyrene circle used for packing pizzas (wiped clean)
- tracing paper and pencil
- scissors
- sticky tape
- 4 wooden skewers about 25 cm long
- 24 cm x 12 cm piece of very thin fabric or a clean, disposable cleaning cloth
- thread

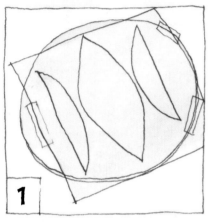

1 Trace the hull templates. Trace the side hull twice. Tape the tracing paper on to the polystyrene. Cut through the paper and polystyrene.

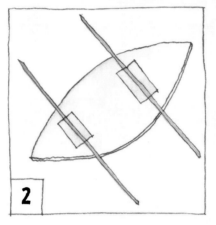

2 Remove the tracing paper. Tape 2 skewers across the centre of the main hull.

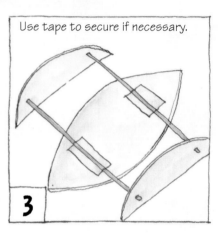

Use tape to secure if necessary.

3 Hold the side hulls with their curved sides upwards and gently push them on to the ends of the skewers.

4 Cut the fabric or cloth into 2 triangles. Thread a skewer up the side of each one. Tie a 20-cm length of thread to each loose corner.

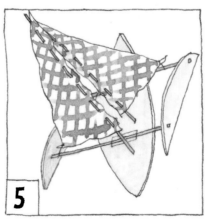

5 Push these 'masts' into the main hull. Tie the loose threads to the horizontal skewers.

6 Tape the 2 masts together at the top. You're ready to sail!

10

Monohulls and Hydrofoils

'Drag' is the force that slows a boat down when it's moving through the water. The less hull a boat has in the water the faster it can go.

A monohull is a boat with one hull. A normal sailing yacht is a monohull and can sail at up to 35 km per hour.

A catamaran has two hulls. When the wind blows strongly it can lean and balance on one hull and go at up to 55 km per hour.

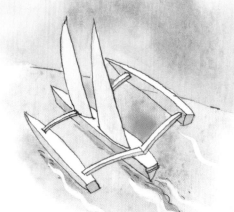

A trimaran has three hulls – one main hull and two 'floats'. In high winds it can speed along on one float at up to 60 km per hour.

A hydrofoil has three hulls and amazing slanting runners under the side hulls. When the wind gets up, all three hulls can be lifted out of the water and the boat speeds along on these runners at up to 66 km per hour.

Weather Station

Be a weather scientist with this handy barometer and rain gauge. The barometer will tell you what the air pressure is like and you'll be able to see how this affects whether it rains or not! Why not keep a record of your findings in a notebook?

Beaker Barometer

If you can't find clear tubing or straws then use a regular stripy straw – the food colouring will help you to see the level of the water.

What you will need:
- clear glass or plastic beaker or jam jar
- sticky tape and ruler
- 20-cm clear plastic tube or drinking straw
- food colouring
- re-usable sticky tack

1 Tape the ruler upright on the outside of the beaker or jar.

2 Half-fill the beaker or jar with cold water and put a few drops of food colouring in it.

3 Tape the tube or straw to the inside of the jar. It should not touch the bottom.

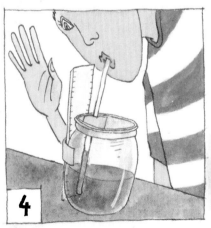

4 Suck some water halfway up the tube. Pinch the tube. Cap the top with sticky tack.

Keep your barometer indoors but make sure it is not in a draughty or sunny place. Note the level of the water in the tube each day, and note if the weather changes.

Rain Catcher

This rain gauge can be hung up over a fence or balcony. Make sure it isn't underneath any overhanging bits of building or roof, or under any trees. Note the level of the water each day in your notebook.

What you will need:

- clean, empty jam jar (preferably with straight sides) or half a clear plastic bottle
- plastic ruler
- re-usable sticky tack
- old wire coathanger

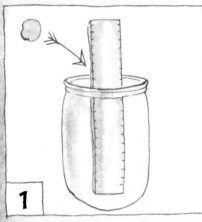

1

Place the ruler inside the jar or bottle half. Secure it to the side of the jar with the sticky tack.

2

Ask a grown-up to help you untwist the wire coathanger and then curl it around the jar or bottle.

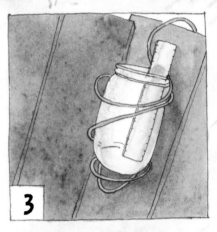

3

Make sure the wire goes underneath the jar or bottle. Finish off with a curl that you can use to hang up the rain gauge.

It's a Fact!

How does your beaker barometer work?

When the pressure in the atmosphere goes up, the water in the barometer jar is forced downwards. This will push the water in the tube or straw upwards. You will see that happening if you check the level against the ruler. Rising atmospheric pressure means that we should have clear or sunny weather.

If the water in the tube is going down this is because the air pressure is going down and could be bringing with it some cloudy or rainy weather.

Snap Happy

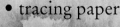

See how a camera works by making this simple device. You'll need a friend to help you.

What you will need:
- old shoe-box or similar
- thick black paint and paintbrush
- pin
- tracing paper
- scissors
- sticky tape
- large, adult-sized coat

Don't make hole too big.

1

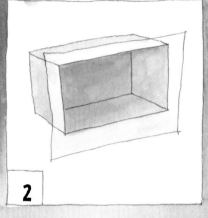

2

3

Take the lid off the box. Paint the inside black and leave it to dry. Use the pin to make a hole in the middle of the bottom of the box.

Cut out a large piece of tracing paper to fit across the open side of the box with about 2 cm to spare on all sides.

Tape the paper firmly around all the sides of the box so that it is stretched tightly across the open side.

Camera Obscura

Camera obscura means 'dark chamber' in Latin. The pinhole camera is a camera obscura on a small scale. But did you know that whole rooms can be made into dark chambers? Artists and astronomers over the centuries have observed images from the outside world through a pinhole of light coming into a specially darkened room.

4 Now you are ready to try out your 'camera'. Take the box and coat outside because it works best in bright light. (If you are inside, point it towards a light or lamp.)

6 Ask a friend to help put the coat over your head and round the sides and bottom of the box. No light should get in!

7 Point the pinhole side of the box at a building or a tree or some other object and you will see an upside-down image of it on the paper screen!

5 Hold the box to your eyes with the tracing paper facing you. Don't press it up to your face, though.

It's a Fact!

Rays of light bounce off the object at which you are pointing the pinhole. These rays carry a picture of it through the pinhole. As these light rays come through the hole they cross over, and so your picture appears upside-down. This is how real cameras see pictures too, except they have film inside them instead of tracing paper!

Your eye is just like a pinhole camera. Luckily your brain unscrambles the pictures you see so that they are the right way up.

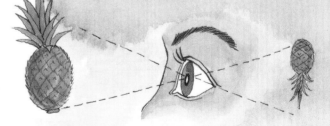

Paddle Power

This wacky, whizzy paddle boat will make bath-time much more fun! You will need to try and find two old pens which are of similar length and weight. Paddle power is another way of seeing Newton's Third Law of Motion in action (see page 4).

What you will need:
- 1 small, empty, plastic bottle with lid
- scissors

- 2 old ballpoint or felt-tip pens
- sticky tape
- elastic band

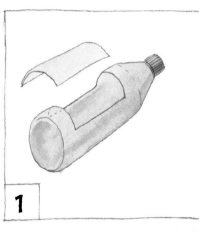

1

Cut a section out of the bottle as shown. Do not throw away the bit you have cut out.

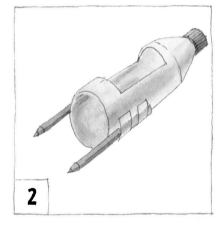

2

Tape the pens to the sides of the bottle. Half of each one should stick out beyond the end of the bottle.

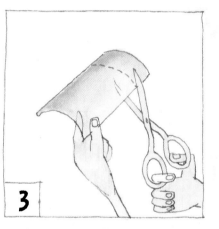

3

Cut a piece of plastic from the strip you have kept. It should be as long as the pen ends and just a bit narrower than the gap between them.

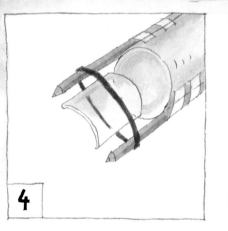

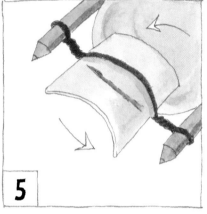

4 Put the elastic band round the pen ends. Place the plastic piece through it with the curved edge facing down.

5 Wind the plastic round and round in an anti-clockwise direction. Twist it as far as it will go.

6 Put the boat in a bath of water and let it go!

Wheels in the Water

Steam engines for ships were first used in paddle boats. The engine turned two massive paddle wheels. The trouble was that these paddle steamers were not much good on the open sea. When there was rough weather the waves lifted one wheel out of the water while the other one was completely submerged. This strained the engine badly. When propellers were invented they were used instead of the paddle wheels because they didn't waste so much of the engine's energy.

Chocks Away!

You could make a few of these cool catapult contraptions and race them with your friends. You'll need to trace the templates on the inside back cover. You can experiment with different-shaped wings, so feel free to adapt these!

What you will need:
- 1 large polystyrene circle used for packing pizzas (wiped clean)
- tracing paper and pencil
- sticky tape
- scissors
- glue or double-sided sticky tape
- 1 paper fastener
- re-usable sticky tack
- elastic band

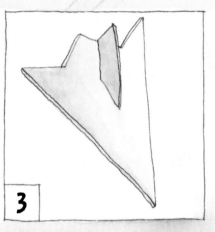

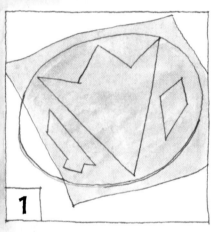

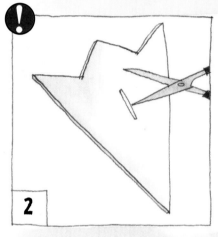

1

Trace the 3 template shapes. Tape the tracing paper on to the polystyrene.

2

Cut through both paper and polystyrene. Cut a slit in the main body as marked on the template.

3

Push the tail piece through the slit so that it stands upright.

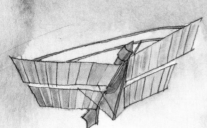

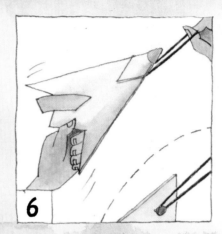

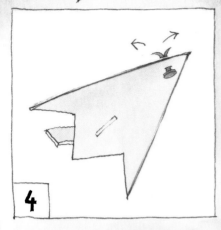

4 Push the paper fastener through the main body near the 'nose'. Fold the 'legs' of the fastener back but make sure the pin head is not too tight up against the polystyrene.

5 Using glue or double-sided tape, fix the small body piece on top of the fastener. Mould a piece of sticky tack around the glider's nose to weight it.

6 Place the elastic band round the head of the fastener. Pull it tight and launch your glider (let go of the tail!)

The Wonderful Wright Brothers

The first people to create a flying machine with an engine – Wilbur and Orville Wright – started with gliders! They created some amazing contraptions. Some of them travelled up to 200 metres but they relied on the wind for power.

The ingenious Wright brothers eventually came up with a flying machine with an engine and two propellers. On 17 December 1903 it took off and flew about 40 metres. It was the world's first powered flight.

Manic Messages

Build a nifty electrical circuit with two switches to control the flashing bulbs and send messages by Morse code. The complete code is on the opposite page. Send a friend into the next room with their half of the circuit. To receive a message you need to hold down your switch while your friend taps their switch off and on to make the bulbs flash. Then you send your answer while your friend holds their switch down.

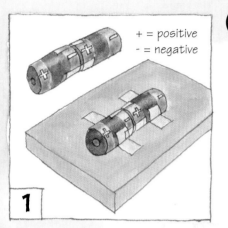

1

Tape the batteries into 2 pairs. Tape them on to the box lids or cardboard. (Put the + and - together as shown.)

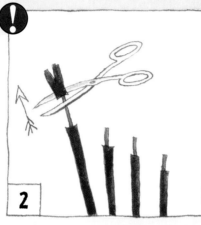

+ = positive
- = negative

2

Using the scissors, strip a small bit of plastic from each end of all the pieces of wire.

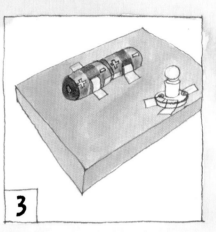

3

Tape the bulb-holders on to the lids or cardboard and screw in the bulbs.

WARNING!
You must NEVER experiment or play with mains electricity from an electrical socket.

5 Fix each end of one 2-metre wire to the batteries with the sticky tack or plasticine.

close-up of switch

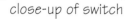
switch

6 Use sticky tack or plasticine to fix one 12-cm wire to each of the other ends of the batteries. Curl the other end round a drawing-pin, and push it through a paper-clip and into the cardboard.

7 Curl each end of the other 2-metre wire under one screw of each bulb-holder and tighten the screws.

What you will need:

- 2 shoe-box lids or pieces of thick cardboard
- 4 x 1.5 volt batteries
- 2 x 2-2.5 v torch bulbs and holders
- 4 x 12-cm lengths of plastic-covered electrical wire
- 2 x 2-metre lengths of plastic-covered electrical wire
- scissors
- re-usable sticky tack or plasticine
- sticky tape
- screwdriver
- 4 drawing-pins
- 2 paper-clips

Use the screwdriver to loosen the screws on each side of the bulb-holders.

Dots and Dashes

Morse code was invented in 1838 by Samuel Morse. He sent a message in the form of electrical signals along a wire. He tapped out long and short sounds to represent different letters of the alphabet. You can do the same by making the light bulbs flash quickly for a dot or longer for a dash.

A • —
B — • • •
C — • — •
D — • •
E •
F • • — •
G — — •
H • • • •
I • •
J • — — —
K — • —
L • — • •
M — —
N — •
O — — —
P • — — •
Q — — • —
R • — •
S • • •
T —
U • • —
V • • • —
W • — —
X — • • —
Y — • — —
Z — — • •

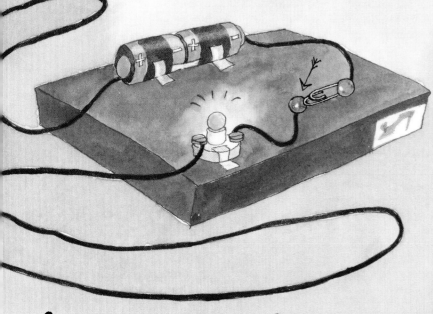

8 Curl the end of a 12-cm wire round a drawing-pin and then push it into the cardboard.

9 Curl the other end of the 12-cm wire under the screws on the other sides of the bulb-holders.

Whizzy Whirler

This is a simple version of a helicopter! Follow the instructions on page 2 to trace the template from the inside front cover on to the card.

What you will need:
- thin card (from a cereal box or similar)
- tracing paper and pencil
- scissors
- drinking straw
- paper-clip
- sticky tape

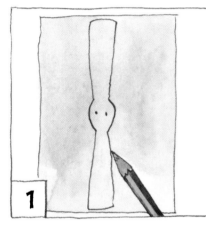

1

Trace the template outline on to the card. Cut it out.

2

Uncurl the paper-clip so that it just has one bend left. Push the ends through the dots in the middle of the propeller.

3

Push the ends down into the straw. Use sticky tape to make the propeller extra secure.

4

Hold the straw between the palms of your hands. Roll the straw between them and then let it go with a throwing motion.

It's a Fact!

Squashed or compressed air helps a helicopter take off. As the blades, or rotors, whiz round they push air down. This squashes the air underneath them, and this compressed air pushes the helicopter upwards.

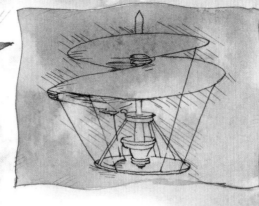

The Ingenious Leonardo

An amazing, early version of a helicopter was designed by Leonardo da Vinci during the fifteenth century. He was a painter, architect, musician and inventor who drew all sorts of designs for many weird and wonderful devices. His 'airscrew' was a corkscrew-shaped contraption. The screw turning would have made it climb upwards like a modern-day helicopter.

Sikorsky's Solution

The first helicopter was invented in 1907 by a Frenchman named Paul Cornu. It had two rotors, and could go up about 2 metres into the air. The trouble was that the body of the helicopter spun round too – in the opposite direction to the wings!
This problem is known as 'torque'.
In 1939 a Russian called Igor Sikorsky designed a helicopter with a main rotor and one at the tail of the machine too. This small rotor solved the problem of 'torque' and kept the body of the helicopter from whirling around at the same time as the wings!

23

Kinetic Capers

A fun and wacky game for two. Make a mad marble run with two columns of toilet roll tubes! The first marble to finish is the winner.

What you will need:
- thin card (from a cereal box or similar)
- 8 toilet roll tubes
- pencil
- scissors
- sticky tape
- a very large sheet of thick cardboard
- double-sided tape
- marbles

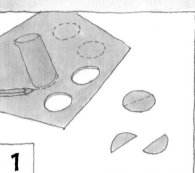

1 Draw 5 circles on the thin card using a tube as a guide. Cut these circles out and then cut them in half.

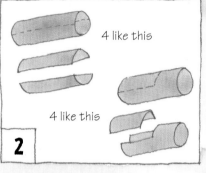

4 like this

4 like this

2 Cut 4 of the toilet roll tubes in half lengthways. Cut the remaining 4 as shown.

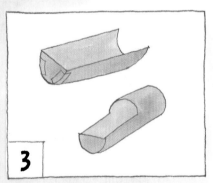

3 Put 2 halves to one side. Tape a half-circle of card to one end of all the other halved or cut rolls.

Ones without half-circles at the top.

4 Use double-sided tape to stick the rolls on to the large piece of cardboard as shown.

It's a Fact!

When you let the marbles go at the top of the 'run' they run down because of the pull of gravity. At the top of the run, before you let them go, the marbles are full of 'potential' energy. Once they are rolling down this energy becomes 'kinetic' energy.